To

_____

From

_____

Date_____

Meditation

The Helen Steiner Rice Foundation

Whatever the celebration, whatever the day, whatever the event, whatever the occasion, Helen Steiner Rice possessed the ability to express the appropriate feeling for that particular moment in time.

A happening became happier, a sentiment more sentimental, a memory more memorable because of her deep sensitivity to put into understandable language the emotion being experienced. Her positive attitude, her concern for others, and her love of God are identifiable threads woven into her life, her works . . . and even her death.

Prior to her passing, she established the HELEN STEINER RICE FOUNDATION, a nonprofit corporation whose purpose is to award grants to worthy charitable programs and aid the elderly, the needy, and the poor. In her lifetime, these were the individuals about whom Mrs. Rice was greatly concerned.

Royalties from the sale of this book will add to the financial capabilities of the HELEN STEINER RICE FOUNDATION. Each year this foundation presents grants to various qualified, worthwhile, and charitable programs. Because of her foresight, her caring, and her deep convictions, Helen Steiner Rice continues to touch a countless number of lives. Thank you for your assistance in helping to keep Helen's dream alive.

Virginia J. Ruehlmann, Administrator
The Helen Steiner Rice Foundation
Suite 2100, Atrium Two
221 East Fourth Street
Cincinnati, Ohio 45202

Precious Moments of

Meditation

Verses by Helen Steiner Rice
Compiled by Virginia J. Ruehlmann
Illustrations by Samuel J. Butcher

Fleming H. Revell
A Division of Baker Book House
Grand Rapids, Michigan 49516

The endsheets,
enhanced with real flower petals,
ferns, and other botanicals,
are from
"The Petals Everlasting Collection"
manufactured by Permalin Products.

Text copyright 1993 by Helen Steiner Rice Foundation
Art copyright 1993 by PRECIOUS MOMENTS, Inc.

Published by Fleming H. Revell,
a division of Baker Book House
P.O. Box 6287, Grand Rapids, Michigan 49516-6287

Library of Congress Cataloging-in-Publication Data

Rice, Helen Steiner.
    Precious moments of meditation / verses by Helen Steiner Rice ; compiled by
Virginia J. Ruehlmann ; illustrations by Samuel J. Butcher.
        p.   cm.
    ISBN 0-8007-1694-9
    1. Christian poetry, American. I. Ruehlmann, Virginia J. II. Butcher, Samuel J.
(Samuel John), 1939–   . III. Title.
PS3568.I28P746   1993
811'.54—dc20   93-6576

Printed in the United States of America

Contents

So we may know God better
and feel His quiet power,
let us daily keep in silence
a meditation hour.

For to understand God's greatness
and to use His gifts each day
the soul must learn to meet Him
in a meditative way.

I come to meet You, God . . .
and as I linger here
I seem to feel You very near.

A rustling leaf
a rolling slope
speaks to my heart of endless hope.

The sun just rising in the sky,
the waking birdlings as they fly,
the grass all wet with morning dew
are telling me I've just met You!

And gently thus the day is born
and night gives way to breaking morn.
And once again I've met You, God,
and worshiped on Your holy sod.
For who can see the dawn break through
without a glimpse of heaven and You?

For who but God could make the day
and softly put the night away?

$\mathcal{E}$ach time you look up in the sky
or watch the fluffy clouds drift by,
or feel the sunshine warm and bright,
or watch the dark night turn to light,

or hear a bluebird gaily sing,
or see the winter turn to spring,
or stop to pick a daffodil,
or gather violets on some hill . . .
or touch a leaf or see a tree,
it's all God whispering, "This is Me . . .
and I am faith
and I am light
and in Me
there shall be no night."

All nature heeds the call of spring
as God awakens everything.
And all that seemed so dead and still
experiences a sudden thrill
as springtime lays a magic hand
across God's vast and fertile land.

Oh, how can anyone stand by
and watch a sapphire springtime sky,
or see a fragile flower break through
what just a day ago or two
seemed barren ground still hard with frost?

14

But in God's world no life is lost,
and flowers sleep beneath the ground.
But when they hear spring's waking sound
they push themselves through layers of clay
to reach the sunlight of God's day.

And man, like flowers, too must sleep
until he is called from the darkened deep
to live in that place where angels sing
and where there is eternal spring!

Hour by hour
and day by day
I talk to God
and say when I pray:
"God, show me the way
so I know what to do.
I am willing and ready
if I just knew
what course to take
and what to say."

But it seems no matter how much I pray
the answer I cannot seem to hear.
And life grows more confused and unclear.
I ask myself,
"Do I hear the Lord's voice
and just refuse
to heed His choice?"

I remember so well this prayer I said each night as my mother tucked me in bed. And today this same prayer is still the best way to sign off with God at the end of the day.

And to ask Him your soul to safely keep
as you wearily close tired eyes in sleep
feeling content that the Father above
will hold you secure in His great arms of love.

And having his promise that if ere you wake
His angels will reach down your sweet soul to take
is perfect assurance that awake or asleep
God is always right there to tenderly keep
all of His children ever safe in His care.

For God's here and He's there, and He's everywhere.
So into His hands each night as I sleep
I commit my soul for the dear Lord to keep.
Knowing that if my soul should take flight,
it will soar to the land where there is no night.

God, be my resting place and my protection
in hours of trouble,

defeat,

and dejection . . .

20

May I never give way to self-pity and sorrow.
May I always be sure of a better tomorrow.

May I stand undaunted, come what may
secure in the knowledge I have only to pray
and ask my Creator and Father above
to keep me serene in His grace and His love!

$\mathcal{G}$od,
help me in my feeble way
to somehow do something each day
to show You
that I love You best
and that my faith will stand each test.

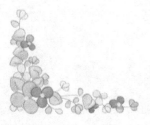

And let me serve You every day
and feel You near me when I pray. . .

Oh, hear my prayer, dear God above,
and make me worthy of Your love!

$\mathcal{I}$ have prayed on my knees in the morning,
I have prayed as I walked along,
I have prayed in the silence and darkness
and I've prayed to the tune of a song.

I have prayed in the midst of triumph
and I've prayed when I suffered defeat,
I have prayed on the sands of the seashore
where the waves of the ocean beat.

I have prayed in a velvet-hushed forest
where the quietness calmed my fears.
I have prayed through suffering and heartache
when my eyes were blinded with tears.

I have prayed in churches and chapels,
cathedrals and synagogues, too.
But often I've had the feeling
that my prayers were not getting through.

And I realized then that our Father
is not really concerned where we pray
or impressed by our manner of worship
or the eloquent words that we say.

He is only concerned with our feelings,
and He looks deep into our heart
and hears the cry of our soul's deep need
that no words could ever impart.

So it isn't the prayer that's expressive
or offered in some special spot.
It's the sincere plea of a sinner
and God can tell whether or not
we honestly seek His forgiveness
and earnestly mean what we say.

And then, and then only, He answers
the prayer that we fervently pray.

I said a little prayer for you
and I asked the Lord above
to keep you safely in His care
and enfold you in His love.

I did not ask for fortune
or riches or for fame.
I only asked for blessings
in the Savior's holy name.

Blessings to surround you
in times of trial and stress.
And inner joy to fill your heart
with peace and happiness.

29

$\mathcal{L}$ord, show me the way
I can somehow repay
the blessings You've given to me.

Lord, teach me to do
what You most want me to
and to be what You want me to be.

I'm unworthy, I know
but I do love You so.
I beg You to answer my plea.

I've not much to give
but as long as I live
may I give it completely to Thee!

God of love—Forgive! Forgive!
Teach us how to truly live.
Ask us not our race or creed,
just take us in our hour of need.

And let us know You love us, too,
and that we are a part of You . . .
and someday may man realize
that all the earth and seas and skies
belong to God, who made us all,
the rich, the poor, the great, the small.

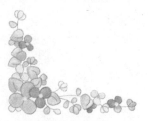

And in the Father's holy sight
no man is yellow, black, or white,
and peace on earth cannot be found
until we meet on common ground.

And every man becomes a brother
who worships God and loves all others.

God knows no stranger.
He loves us all.
The poor, the rich,
the great, the small.
He is a friend
who is always there
to share our troubles
and lessen our care.

No one is a stranger in God's sight.
For God is love
and in His light
may we, too, try
in our small way
to make new friends
from day to day.

So pass no stranger
with an unseeing eye.
For God may be sending
a new friend by.

$\mathscr{T}$ake me
and break me
and make me,
dear God,
just what You want me to be.

Give me the strength to accept what You send
and eyes with the vision to see
all the small, arrogant ways that I have
and the vain little things that I do.

Make me aware that I'm often concerned
more with myself than with You.
Uncover before me my weakness and greed
and help me to search deep inside
so I may discover how easy it is
to be selfishly lost in my pride.

And then in Your goodness and mercy
look down on this weak, erring one
and tell me that I am forgiven
for all I've so willfully done.

And teach me to humbly start following
the path that the dear Savior trod.
So I'll find at the end of life's journey
a home in the City of God.

God, grant us hope
and faith
and love.

Hope for a world
grown cynically cold,
hungry for power,
and greedy for gold.

Faith to believe
when within and without
there's a nameless fear
in a world of doubt.

Love that is bigger
than race or creed,
to cover the world
and fulfill each need.

The future
is not ours to know
and it may never be.
So let us live
and give our best
and give it lavishly.

And let us be content to solve
our problems
one by one.
Asking nothing
of tomorrow except
"Thy will be done."

"Make me a channel of blessing today,"
I ask again and again
when I pray.

Do I turn a deaf ear to the Master's voice
or refuse to heed His directions and choice?

I only know at the end of the day
That I did so little to
                    "pay
                          my
                                way"!

We all have cares and problems
we cannot solve alone.
But if we go to God in prayer
we are never on our own . . .

And if we try to stand alone
we are weak and will fall,
for God is always greatest
when we're helpless, lost, and small.

And no day is unmeetable
if on rising, our first thought
is to thank God for the blessings
that His loving care has brought . . .

For there can be no failures
or hopeless, unsaved sinners
if we enlist the help of God
who makes all losers winners.

We cannot all be famous
or be listed in "Who's Who."
But every person great or small
has important work to do.

For seldom do we realize
the importance of small deeds
or to what degree of greatness
unnoticed kindness leads.

For it's not the big celebrity
in a world of fame and praise,
but it's doing unpretentiously
in undistinguished ways

55

The work that God assigned to us,
unimportant as it seems,
that makes our task outstanding
and brings reality to dreams.

So do not sit and idly wish
for wider, new dimensions
where you can put in practice
your many good intentions.

But at the spot God placed you
begin at once to do
the little things to brighten up
the lives surrounding you.

For if everybody brightened up
the spot on which they're standing
by being more considerate
and a little less demanding

This dark old world would very soon
eclipse the evening star
if everybody brightened up
the corner where they are!

We are all God's children
and He loves us everyone.
He freely and completely
forgives all that we have done.

Asking only if we're ready
to follow where He leads,
content that in His wisdom
He will answer all our needs.

*P*rayers for big and little things
fly heavenward on angels' wings.
And He who walked by the Galilee
and touched the blind and made them see,
and cured the man who long was lame
when he but called God's holy name,
will keep you safely in His care
and when you need Him,
He'll be there!

There's only one place
and only one friend
who is never too busy
and you can always depend
that He will be waiting
with arms open wide
to hear all your troubles
that you care to confide.

For the heavenly Father
will always be there
when you seek Him and find Him
at the altar of prayer.